Fasting for Breakthrough

Break Chains. Destroy Yokes. Walk in Freedom.

Calvin M. Blake II

MHB
PUBLISHING
COMPANY

MHB Publishing Company
Georgia, USA

www.mhbpublishingcompany.com

MHB
PUBLISHING
COMPANY

Scripture quotations taken from the Holy Bible, New International Version (NIV), New Living Translation (NLT), The Message (MSG), Amplified Bible (AMP) and New American Standard Bible (NASB).

Printed in the United States of America.

ISBN: 9798999659910

First and foremost, I dedicate this work, this masterpiece to **God**, who is my Father, my Rock, my Redeemer, and my Sustainer. Without His grace, wisdom, and unfailing love, this book would not even exist. Every page is a reflection of His power to transform, to heal, and to break the chains that hold His people captive. May this offering of sacrifice bring glory to His name and point every reader back to the One who still sets captives free.

I also dedicate this book to the memory of my late father, **Calvin M. Blake, Sr.,** whose legacy of faith continues to inspire me, and to my loving mother, **Sandra D. Blake**, whose prayers, encouragement, and steadfast faith have been a constant anchor in my life. To my beloved wife, **Mary H. Blake**, whose unwavering love, prayers, and support are a constant source of strength. To my daughter, **Krystal Tucker**, and my son, **Isaiah Blake**—you are my joy, my legacy, and my motivation to keep pressing forward in the work of the Lord.

Lastly, to my precious grandson, **Jayce Tucker**, may you grow to know and serve the God who breaks every chain. May your life be a testimony of His goodness and power. This book is a labor of love for my family and for the Kingdom, written so that generations to come will know that fasting, when done in faith, is a mighty weapon in the hands of God's people.

Contents

Book Forward by Mary H. Blake

IT BRINGS ME IMMENSE PLEASURE TO FORWARD THIS BOOK.

My husband Calvin M. Blake, II, encourages me to be the best version of the me that God sees. I can honestly say that throughout the 24 years of marriage, this man has taught and shown me what truly serving God looks like. I mean, truly, what it looks! He does not portray himself as being one person in front of people, then has another face behind closed doors. From the very start, his heart is and have been pure for God. His desire is to serve God and love God's people is what propels him forward in every circumstance in life, good or bad.

Fasting has been a part of Calvin's life for as long as I can remember. I remember several series of 3-day dry fasts with no food, no water, I mean nothing! Those days were certainly long, but I knew for him they were worth it. While Calvin has always incorporated fasting as part of his life, his reason and focus behind the fasting has always been the same—God. The commitment behind it must be God. Fasting is one of those things that you must hear from God and be instructed to do. It brings about impressive results if you do it the correct way. We have led our ministry of many years through fasting and praying, to bring about change in the lives of God's servants.

I like to stand on the scripture:

Ezra 8:21- *Then I proclaimed a fast there at the river of Ahava, that we might humble ourselves before our God, to seek from Him the right way for us and our little ones and all our possessions.*

I am honored to have witnessed my husband share what God has given him through his first book, and to have published it through my company. This book is a great tool to help you start and complete your fast in God. Fasting for God will allow you to grow and mature in the things of God. Use this book as a guide to support you in your journey as you continue to commit and fully surrender to God. This is just the beginning of God doing new things in your life.

God Bless,

Pastor Mary H. Blake - Author, Chief Editor & Founder of MHB Publishing Company

Introduction

DO YOU KNOW HOW IMPORTANT YOU ARE TO THE LORD?

You are the greatest person God has put on this earth. As a matter of fact, the bible declares in **Isaiah 43:4** that, *"You are precious to me. You are honored, and I love you.."* Wow!!!

Such loving words from a loving father. So that goes without saying that you are not an accident, you are not overlooked, nor are you forgotten. The problem becomes that we don't see ourselves the same way the father sees us. We believed what the enemy said about us and are reduced to living to survive, maintaining, and getting by. We've lost our ambition and drive to be everything God has called us to be, and we are okay with that. But not so, it's time we turn the tables on the enemy and take our life back and assume our place of authority. Taking back your life begins now!!! We are calling out every lie of the enemy, getting rid of every label attached to you, and every limitation that has made you feel unworthy.

Not only are you going to live, but you are going to feel alive again. What God has in store for you exceeds your current situation, your past pain, or even your greatest imagination. Oh, you may not feel it right now. You may not even see it yet, but God is preparing something *eternal, beautiful, and purposeful* — just for you.

Now, in order for our life to align with God and his word, we must go back to what works and has always worked, **fasting and praying**.

The bible opens up and declares the phrase in **Matthew 6:16**, *"When you fast"*. According to this passage of text, Jesus is emphasizing that fasting is expected in the life of a believer — not optional.

The bible also teaches us in **Luke 18:1** that, *"Men ought to always pray and not to faint."* Jesus is giving his stance on persistent prayer and encouraging believers to keep praying, even when answers seem delayed. So, know fasting and praying work. They cure unbelief, they get rid of the strongholds of this world that have had an influence on your life so that you can experience breath through and not only be but become everything God has called you to be. Come take a journey with me for the next 21 days as we take our life back and align it with God.

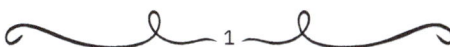

Fasting leads to essential promises of God

✳ **Being Healed**

✳ **Being Delivered**

✳ **Being Set Free**

Each section offers a brief guide backed by the word of God, to help you tap into the life-changing work of Jesus Christ.

Being Healed

Why Healing Matters

God's heart is to restore our wholeness—body, soul, and spirit. When we fast, we partner with Him in prayer, opening ourselves up intimately for Him to minister to our deepest hurts.

Guidelines for Healing: Acknowledge Your Need

"Heal me, O Lord, and I shall be healed; save me, and I shall be saved, for you are my praise." **Jeremiah 17:14**

☐ **Confess and Repent**
"If we confess our sins, he is faithful and just to forgive us our sins..." **1 John 1:9**

☐ **Claim God's Promises**
"By his stripes you were healed."**Isaiah 53:5** and **1 Peter 2:24**

☐ **Meditate on His Word**
"My son, pay attention to my words; incline your ear to my sayings. Let them not escape from your sight; keep them within your heart..." **Proverbs 4:20-21**

☐ **Fast with Faith**
Set aside food and comfort items for a time period. Replace this time with prayer and scripture meditation. Declare God's healing over your body and mind until break through manifests.

Fasting leads to essential promises of God

Being Delivered

The Need for Deliverance

Strongholds of fear, addiction, bitterness, or even oppression can bind us and keep us away from truth and knowing the truth, who is Jesus Christ. Deliverance releases us from spiritual bondage and restores our authority in Jesus Christ.

Guidelines for Deliverance

☐ **Recognize the Bondage**

"For though we walk in the flesh, we are not waging war according to the flesh." **2 Corinthians 10:3**

☐ **Submit to God**

"Submit yourselves therefore to God. Resist the devil, and he will flee from you." **James 4:7**

☐ **Use the Name of Jesus**

"And whatever you ask in my name, that I will do..." **John 14:13**

☐ **Break Yokes in Prayer**

"Is not this the fast that I choose: to loose the bonds of wickedness, to undo the straps of the yoke..." **Isaiah 58:6**

☐ **Declare Freedom**

Speak aloud in faith: "I cancel every assignment of the enemy against me. I am delivered and will never be bound again in Jesus' name!"

Fasting leads to essential promises of God

Being Set Free

Living in Freedom

True freedom isn't just release from chains—it's walking daily in the life and authority Jesus bought for us and made available to us.

Guidelines for Walking in Freedom

☐ **Put on the New Self**
"Put on the new self, created after the likeness of God in true righteousness and holiness." **Ephesians 4:24**

☐ **Walk by the Spirit**
"If we live by the Spirit, let us also keep in step with the Spirit."
Galatians 5:25

☐ **Guard Your Heart**
"Above all else, guard your heart, for everything you do flows from it."
Proverbs 4:23

☐ **Worship and Praise**
"The Lord is near to the brokenhearted and saves the crushed in spirit."
Psalm 34:18

☐ **Persevere in Prayer**
Maintain a lifestyle of fasting and prayer. Celebrate being set free and keep declaring the truth of God's Word over your life.

Note:

As you fast and follow these guidelines, expect transformation, expect change, expect to see the you God called to come forth. God is faithful to heal, deliver, and set you free from everything. May this journey draw you deeper into His glorious presence—and into the abundant life he has promised for you.

Keys to Fasting

Fasting is something that we should never enter or take lightly. The main purpose of fasting is to cure you from unbelief and to bring you closer to God. Fasting allows your faith to come alive so that we will believe everything that is written in God's Word.

Here are some tips for fasting effectively in God, to gain the spiritual success and have an effective fast.

Plan & Prepare:

Choose the Type of Fast:
Decide on the type of fast that aligns with your spiritual goals and health needs. Common types include a total fast (abstaining from all food and drink), a partial fast (restricting certain foods or meals), or a Daniel fast (eating only fruits and vegetables).

- **Create a Schedule:**
Determine the duration of your fast (e.g., one day, a week, or longer) and plan how you will manage it day-to-day. Consider how you will handle meals, social situations, and any potential challenges.

- **Prepare Mentally and Physically:**
Gradually adjust your diet leading up to the fast to ease the transition. Mentally prepare by focusing on your spiritual intentions and any supportive practices like prayer, meditation, or scripture reading.

- **Reflect on what it is you are seeking God for:**
Begin by setting aside time for reflection and prayer. Seek clarity on why you want to fast and what you hope to achieve spiritually. This could involve drawing closer to God, seeking guidance, or deepening your understanding of your faith.

Keys to Fasting

Create Spiritual Practices

- **Pray, Pray, Pray:**

Prayer is key when starting any fast. Instead of focusing on what you will eat substitute mealtime for prayer, meditation, or reading God's word. This helps to keep your focus on the spiritual aspects of the fast rather than physical hunger.

- **Journal and Reflect:**

Keep a journal to document your experiences, thoughts, and awareness gained during your fast. Reflect on how you are moving towards your goals and any changes you notice in your spiritual life. Write down the things you are praying and believing God to do or change.

- **Get in Your Word:**

Reading your word is key to succeeding in fasting. Turn off the TV's, radios, social media, then commit yourself to read God's word. God's word will come alive to you when you fast. Allow the Holy Spirit to guide you. Trust and believe that the words that you read are True. If that does not work, start with the readings of Christ Jesus. The Book of John is a beautiful place to start when wanting to learn more of Christ works on the earth.

Principle Fasting Scriptures

"Even now," declares the Lord, "return to me with all your heart, with fasting and weeping and mourning." **Joel 2:12**

Key Insight: Fasting is a call to return, to repent, and to realign with God's heart.

"So, we fasted and petitioned our God about this, and he answered our prayer." **Ezra 8:23**

Key Insight: Fasting positions you to hear clearly and receive divine assistance.

"Go, gather all the Jews... and fast for me... I will go to the king... And if I perish, I perish" **Esther 4:16**

Key Insight: Fasting prepares you for courage, favor, and supernatural intervention.

"While they were worshiping the Lord and fasting, the Holy Spirit said, 'Set apart for me Barnabas and Saul...'" **Acts 13:2-3**

Key Insight: Fasting creates space for God to speak and send with purpose

"However, this kind does not go out except by prayer and fasting." **Matthew 17:21**

Key Insight: Some spiritual resistance requires the deeper sacrifice and focus of fasting.

"At that time, I, Daniel, mourned for three weeks. I ate no choice food; no meat or wine touched my lips..." **Daniel 10:2-3**

Key Insight: Fasting prepares the spirit to receive divine revelation and angelic visitation.

"When I heard these things, I sat down and wept. For some days I mourned and fasted and prayed before the God of heaven." **Nehemiah 1:4**

Key Insight: Fasting is a godly response to crisis and can stir divine strategies.

How to Know if Your Fast is Effective

1. You're Becoming Spiritually Sensitive

"Man shall not live by bread alone, but by every word that proceeds from the mouth of God." **Matthew 4:4**

Evidence: You hear God's voice more clearly, Scripture hits deeper, dreams become more vivid, or you begin to sense spiritual things more easily. This is a sign that your spiritual appetite is overtaking your natural one.

2. You're Experiencing Conviction, Not Just Emotion

"Return to Me with all your heart, with fasting..." **Joel 2:12**

Evidence: God begins to highlight hidden areas — pride, bitterness, fear, distraction — not to condemn you, but to cleanse and realign you.

3. You're Developing Discipline Over Desires

"I discipline my body and bring it into subjection..." **1 Corinthians 9:27**

Evidence: You begin to gain control over your cravings, emotions, and impulses. What once had control over you now begins to lose power.

4. You're Receiving Clarity and Direction

"While they were worshiping the Lord and fasting, the Holy Spirit said..." **Acts 13:2**

Evidence: You start receiving instructions, confirmations, open doors, or unexpected insight — often connected to what you've been praying about.

5. You Feel Resistance

"This kind comes out only by prayer and fasting." **Matthew 17:21**

Evidence: Sometimes, spiritual warfare intensifies. If you feel heaviness, distraction, or even unusual opposition — it's a sign your fast is threatening enemy territory. Don't quit — push through. The pressure is often proof something is about to break.

6. You Notice Divine Appointments or Unusual Peace

"And the peace of God... will guard your hearts and minds..." **Philippians 4:7**

Evidence: Unexpected doors open. People or opportunities appear. Or, in the absence of visible change, you feel a supernatural calm that God is working behind the scenes.

How to Know if Your Fast is Effective

7. You Feel an Inner Shift — Even Without Outer Change Being Evident

"They that wait on the Lord shall renew their strength..." **Isaiah 40:31**

Evidence: Even if nothing changes outwardly, your faith is rising, your mind is sharpening, and your spirit is strengthening. You're becoming prepared for the manifestation. Are you ready for the next 21 Days? Because this journey is absolutely necessary. By reading this book, you will have a better understanding of God's entire plan for your life and how God intends for you to live while here on earth, as a Kingdom Citizen. Let's take this one day at a time and watch how God unfolds your life.

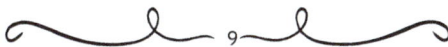

Being Healed Through Fasting

Being Healed Through Fasting

You know, let's first begin by establishing the fact that fasting is more than skipping meals—it's an invitation for God to take center stage in your life. When we fast with the right heart, we're giving God permission to step into the deepest parts of our being. Healing doesn't always start on the outside—*it starts from within.* That is how we live our lives, from within. And because of this inward living, so many things surface that must be dealt with. The bible declares in **Isaiah 58** that when we fast the way God intended, our healing springs forth speedily. Denying this body is what allows his body to be manifested in us. That's a promise and that's our reality.

Now listen, there's a cleansing that happens when you fast. The Holy Spirit begins to sweep out the corners of our soul where things have been buried such as childhood trauma, relationships, and family unforgiveness, hidden and secret sins. And when those things are brought into the light, healing can begin. The bible declares in **Joel 2**, *"Return to Me with all your heart, with fasting and weeping."* Fasting brings repentance to the surface of your life, not shame and embarrassment for what you did wrong, but restoration and recovery. And once repentance has had its work, healing can flow freely like water from a pure fountain.

Understand that physically, fasting resets the body. And you need to know, your body is the temple of the Holy Ghost. When you fast, you're giving your body time to repair, time to heal, time to regroup and you're inviting the healing power of God to work unhindered in every aspect of life in Christ. Daniel fasted, and the Bible says he appeared healthier and stronger than those who ate from the king's table. That wasn't about diet, it was about consecration, time spent with the Lord and his earnestness for God to be his Lord. You'd be amazed what your body can release when your spirit is aligned and in tune with God. But I want you to know something deeper: Some sicknesses are not physical, they are spiritual. That's why Jesus told his disciples, "This kind comes out only by prayer and fasting." Sometimes, healing won't come until the spirit behind the infirmity is confronted. It is through fasting that you must be okay to confront anything that is blocking you from receiving your healing. Fasting strengthens your authority to cast out what medicine can't diagnose. If it's demonic, if it's generational, if it's spiritual bondage —fasting loses the chains and brings for deliverance.

Now hear me well—fasting is also an *act of faith*. Every time you push away that plate, you're saying, "God, I believe You more than my flesh. I trust You to sustain me." Just like the woman with the issue of blood believed if she touched Jesus, she'd be healed, your fast is your reach. It's how you achieve victory over this body. It's your press through the crowd of distractions, emotions, and limitations. And when God sees your faith, He must respond. So, when you fast, don't just fast for relief—fast for wholeness. Fast to be made complete. Because in that secret place of surrender, that's where healing flows the deepest and you will experience God's transformative power to manifest himself in your life.

Now, let's take the first 7 Days and be totally healed through fasting.

Fasting Guide: Day One

Focus Scripture: Psalms 46:1-11

God is our refuge and strength, a
helper who is always found in
times of trouble.
Therefore, we will not be afraid,
though the earth trembles
and the mountains topple into
the depths of the seas,
though its water roars and foams
and the mountains quake with its turmoilSelah

There is a river— its streams delight the city of
God, the holy dwelling place of the Most High.

God is within her; she will not be toppled.
God will help her when the morning dawns.
Nations rage, kingdoms topple;
the earth melts when he lifts his voice.
The LORD of Armies is with us; the God
of Jacob is our stronghold. Selah

Come, see the works of the LORD,
who brings devastation on the earth. He makes wars
cease throughout the earth. He shatters bows and
cuts spears to pieces; he sets wagons ablaze. "Stop
fighting, and know that I am God, exalted among the
nations, exalted on the earth."

The LORD of Armies is with us;
the God of Jacob is our stronghold. Selah

Note:

Use this simple daily focus as a heartbeat for your fast: Set yourself apart, turn from every
weight, receive Christ's healing, renounce every chain, embrace your true identity, walk in
Spirit-given authority, and celebrate the freedom Jesus secured for you. Let each day begin
with this anchor verse—spoken out loud, prayed back to God, and woven into every choice
you make that day—so that by week's end the rhythm of breakthrough is no longer an event
but a lifestyle.

Guiding Points & Prayer

Note:
Remember to make the text personal, the goal is to use the scriptures to grow stronger in your relationship with Christ. As you approach the day to study, focus on these points in the text.

First Point:

God Is: Notice the number of times the scripture states, "God is." Take the time to reflect and journal what God is to you and who God is to you. Consider how having a relationship with God has changed your life internally and externally. It is of utter importance that we never take God out of the equations of our lives. We must depend upon him solely for everything. Fasting draws us into the refuge of where healing begins because God is our strength. Even when everything shakes, He is present, and His presence restores. That's who God is.

Second Point:

You can face it: Notice the obstacles in the text, see how God is seen with a counter action for every instance stated. As you are in prayer, deal with your past fears and all the things that come to limit you. Fasting gives you the strength to face what once made you run, because God is your refuge and help. In His presence, you don't have to fear the storm, He heals you in the middle of it. Recall the times how God showed up to intervene, be it great or small and remember you were given the strength to face it and win.

Final Point:

God's Faithfulness: Remembering God's faithfulness in times of trouble and difficulties can be exceedingly difficult while you are in the thicket of it all. Think on a time when God showed himself dependable, trustworthy, and dependable. How did that make you feel? What was your response to God? Did it change or alter your view of God? Fasting reveals the faithfulness of a God who is present in every trouble and near in every wound. Healing comes not because we are strong, but because He is always faithful and will remain faithful.

Prayer:

Dear God, I acknowledge you today. I thank you for your constant love and never- ending grace. Thank you for your strength, I acknowledge my need for you in my life today. Thank you, Lord, who makes life easier. Lord, as I fast, be my refuge and strength, my ever-present help in everyplace I hurt. Let Your faithfulness heal the wounds I've carried in silence. Life gets easier when I know that you are leading me.

Date : ___/___/___

_____
_____
_____
_____
_____
_____
_____
_____
_____
_____
_____
_____
_____
_____
_____
_____
_____
_____
_____
_____

Fast That Breaks

Fasting Guide: Day Two

Focus Scripture: 1 Timothy 4:16

Take heed to yourself and to the
doctrine. Continue in them, for in
doing this you will save both you and
those who hear you.

Note:

Use this simple daily focus as a heartbeat for your fast: Set yourself apart, turn from every weight, receive Christ's healing, renounce every chain, embrace your true identity, walk in Spirit-given authority, and celebrate the freedom Jesus secured for you. Let each day begin with this anchor verse—spoken out loud, prayed back to God, and woven into every choice you make that day—so that by week's end the rhythm of breakthrough is no longer an event but a lifestyle.

Guiding Points & Prayer

Note:
Remember to keep a close watch on yourself and on the teachings. Persist in this, as you will save yourself and those around you. As you approach the day to study, focus on these points in the text.

First Point:

Time out: Take this time to examine yourself, your thoughts, your attitude, your actions, and your life. Make sure you are aligned with the word of God. Examine your heart, look for areas of your life that you need God to heal. Fasting is a time-out to watch over your life and your doctrine with fresh eyes. Healing begins when you pause long enough to let God realign what's been overlooked. Take off all layers your lifestyle, does it match with Christ' example?

Second Point:

Be persistent: Chase after God. Put the time in. Make sacrifices in your life to follow him. When you make Godly sacrifices and live a surrendered life, they help you stay aligned with God's word. Fasting teaches us to be persistent in both discipline and faith, even when healing takes time. As you continue the work of being persistent in pursing God, he completes the work, in body, soul, and spirit.

Final Point:

You are being watched: You must be that Godly example in its purest form. This is soul winning! People can be saved just by looking at your life. Don't compromise! Stay focused on living your life out loud so others will see the God in you and want to know more about Christ. As you spend time in prayer, pray for your relationships to be healed. Fasting refines not just your walk, but your witness because someone is watching your healing unfold. As you yield to God, your persistence becomes someone else's hope. Pray that God remain the person that they see and not you.

Prayer:

Dear Lord, in you I exist today. I praise you for being an example on the earth. Forgive my failures and me not trusting you through the process of life. Thank you for never giving up on me and guiding me. Let healing flow through my persistence, that both I and those watching will be made whole. Thank you for the strength to change and become everything you have designed me to be.

Date : ___/___/___

Fasting Guide: Day Three

Focus Scripture: Job 33:14

For God may speak in one way,
or in another,
Yet man does not
perceive it.

Note:

Use this simple daily focus as a heartbeat for your fast: Set yourself apart, turn from every weight, receive Christ's healing, renounce every chain, embrace your true identity, walk in Spirit-given authority, and celebrate the freedom Jesus secured for you. Let each day begin with this anchor verse—spoken out loud, prayed back to God, and woven into every choice you make that day—so that by week's end the rhythm of breakthrough is no longer an event but a lifestyle.

Guiding Points & Prayer

Note:

Remember to know that indeed, God speaks once, or twice, yet no one notices it. As you approach the day to study, focus on these points in the text.

First Point:

God does speak: Be open to hear God speak to you in numerous ways. He can speak through dreams, through people, and even circumstances. Your openness to God releases an availability for conversation. Fasting silences the noise so you can hear the God who still speaks in hidden ways. Healing begins when His voice reaches the place pain has silenced.

Second Point:

God always answers one way or another: His response may be yes, no, wait, not now, or stand still. You must be open and obedient to what he says. Sometimes it's hard to accept to what God says, but the fact that he speaks brings resolution to any matter of the heart. Fasting opens our spirit to recognize the many ways God responds, whether it is through whispers, visions, or silence. One way or another, He speaks healing into every surrendered place.

Final Point:

Relationships exist when there is communication: God needs a partner. The reason we fail to know God's ability to speak, and answer is because the other voices with which we are familiar. This is not a natural relationship. You are in a relationship with the God of heaven. He wants you to have all things, know all things, and become everything he created you to be. Fasting restores communication with the God who still speaks because healing begins with relationship. When you open your heart to listen, he opens His mouth to restore. As you spend time in prayer, pray for your ears and eyes to remain open to the leading of God. Let God direct and lead your life to a life that is pattern after him.

Prayer:

Loving God, I greet you with Worship and Praise. Create in me a heart that wants to commit and communicate with you daily. I surrender my life to you and give you my full heart today. Lord, as I fast, open my ears to hear the way You choose to speak. Heal me through every word You whisper, for I know Your voice brings life. Teach me how to Listen and attend to your word.

Date : ___/___/___

_____
_____
_____
_____
_____
_____
_____
_____
_____
_____
_____
_____
_____
_____
_____
_____
_____
_____
_____
_____

Fast That Breaks

Fasting Guide: Day Four

Focus Scripture: Colossians 2:6-7

So then, just as you received Christ Jesus
as Lord, continue to live your lives in
him, rooted, and built up in him,
strengthened in the faith as you were
taught, and overflowing with
thankfulness.

Note:

Use this simple daily focus as a heartbeat for your fast: Set yourself apart, turn from every weight, receive Christ's healing, renounce every chain, embrace your true identity, walk in Spirit-given authority, and celebrate the freedom Jesus secured for you. Let each day begin with this anchor verse—spoken out loud, prayed back to God, and woven into every choice you make that day—so that by week's end the rhythm of breakthrough is no longer an event but a lifestyle.

Guiding Points & Prayer

Note:

As you search your heart today, in preparation for God to speak, lean your ear to his voice. As you approach the day to study, focus on these points in the text.

First Point:

Receive Christ: Daily, we must receive Christ. That means we must receive his love, his grace, his Spirit leading, his strength, and his peace. Fasting deepens the roots of Christ we've received, anchoring us in His healing power. As we are built up in Him, wholeness begins to rise from the inside out. That we may live as effective stewards and witnesses for him.

Second Point:

Uproot and replant: The hardest part of receiving Christ is having to make changes. You must be willing to uproot, pull up everything that does not look like the Christ you have received. You must replant good seeds of righteousness, seeds of faith, seeds of holiness, seeds of love, and seeds of God's word. Fasting allows God to uproot what was planted in pain and replant me in Christ's truth. Healing begins when old roots are torn out and new life takes hold of Him.

Final Point:

It's time to build: You must know that you are building on a firm foundation. You are building upon the seeds you have planted; therefore, growth is imminent and will take place. Fasting clears the ground so healing can lay a firm foundation in Christ. It's time to build, not on pain, but on the One who restores and makes all things new.

Prayer:

Today, Father, I acknowledge that it is in you that all things exist. I rest in your strength and stand in your power. Build me up in Faith to believe you for all things in your word. Lord, as I fast, root me deeper in Christ and build me stronger in your truth. Let healing flow from every place You restore and establish in your righteousness.

Fast That Breaks

Focus Scripture: Hebrews 11:1

Now faith is confidence in what we
hope for and assurance about what we
do not see.

Note:

Use this simple daily focus as a heartbeat for your fast: Set yourself apart, turn from every weight, receive Christ's healing, renounce every chain, embrace your true identity, walk in Spirit-given authority, and celebrate the freedom Jesus secured for you. Let each day begin with this anchor verse—spoken out loud, prayed back to God, and woven into every choice you make that day—so that by week's end the rhythm of breakthrough is no longer an event but a lifestyle.

Guiding Points & Prayer

Note:
Remember as you fast that faith start with having confidence in God. As you approach the day to study, focus on these points in the text.

First Point:

You will have the evidence: Many assume that seeing is believing. Not so, in Christ seeing is not believing. God will give you the evidence or the sign that whatever you are praying for does exist in the spiritual realm. Fasting fuels the faith that healing is already at work, even before I see it. What begins in hope will end in evidence because God always honors faith. The evidence will show up before the manifestation.

Second Point:

Don't be troubled: Just because you do not see it, should not affect your faith to believe God for it. Trouble has a way of shaking our evidence, delaying manifestation. God does not want you troubled; he wants you trusting in him to believe that faith causes all things to exist in him. Fasting anchors your faith when your feelings want to shake you. I may not see it yet, but healing is the substance I'm standing on, so I won't be troubled.

Final Point:

Now Faith: Let your NOW Faith remain active and strong. Keep believing in God for the impossible to take place. Remember, you don't have to see it, just believe it. Your Deliverance is real; your healing is real. Step back and see how God has changed your life from the inside out. Then you will see the fruits that God sees as a changed Child of God. Fasting activates your now faith, believing that healing isn't coming later, it's moving now. In the silence of sacrifice, God is already working the unseen into reality.

Prayer:

Holy and Majestic God, I thank you for always knowing what is best for me. Thank you for releasing my heart to believe in the impossible. For I know, with you all things are possible. Lord, as I fast, let my now faith rise above what I feel or see. I trust that healing is already taking place because your word is my evidence. Lord, I believe. Thank you for changing my life. I rest in your words and move forward in your strength.

Date : ___/___/___

_____
_____
_____
_____
_____
_____
_____
_____
_____
_____
_____
_____
_____
_____
_____
_____
_____
_____
_____
_____

Fast That Breaks

Fasting Guide: Day Six

Focus Scripture: Exodus 14:14

The Lord will fight for you, and you
shall hold your peace.

Note:

Use this simple daily focus as a heartbeat for your fast: Set yourself apart, turn from every weight, receive Christ's healing, renounce every chain, embrace your true identity, walk in Spirit-given authority, and celebrate the freedom Jesus secured for you. Let each day begin with this anchor verse—spoken out loud, prayed back to God, and woven into every choice you make that day—so that by week's end the rhythm of breakthrough is no longer an event but a lifestyle.

Guiding Points & Prayer

Note:
Learning to embrace God's love and his ability to show up for you. As you approach the day to study, focus on these points in the text.

First Point:

The Lord will: You must commit this to heart. You must be assured of who is going to do it and what He is well capable of doing. The Lord will do what you have asked of Him and more. Fasting teaches us to be still while God does what we thought was impossible. The Lord will fight for your healing, and in His hands, wholeness is guaranteed.

Second Point:

Embrace the fight: Do you know that every race has a finish line? It is hard to see the finish line when everything comes against you all at once. But do not let your current pain spoil your future victory. This is a true race, you must build endurance and strength to make it to the end. Fasting isn't running from the battle; it's standing still and letting God take over. When you embrace the fight His way, healing becomes your victory, not your burden.

Final Point:

Only be silent: Far too often, we can interfere in God's outcome. Being silent doesn't mean I don't have a voice; it simply means I choose to stand in a place of trust with God. You must learn to train and discipline yourself to trust in God, rather than trusting in yourself. Fasting quiets the noise so you can hear the One who heals without striving. In the silence, God fights for you and healing flows where words once got in the way. The confidence of our faith is knowing the power of our God, that He can, and He will. When you take the stand to be silent before God, you will always walk in Victory.

Prayer:

Faithful God, my heart is in your hands. Lead me and guide me through life's difficulties. Let me hide in your word and always speak the truth of your Word. Lord, as I fast, teach me to be still and trust your hand to fight for my healing. In the quiet, let your power speak and make me whole. Help me trust your will and say what you spoke in your word.

Date : ___/___/___

_____
_____
_____
_____
_____
_____
_____
_____
_____
_____
_____
_____
_____
_____
_____
_____
_____
_____
_____
_____
_____
_____
_____
_____

Fast That Breaks

Fasting Guide: Day Seven

Focus Scripture: Psalms 3:2-3

Many are saying of me, "God will not deliver him.". But you Lord are a shield around me, the One who lifts my head high.

Note:

Use this simple daily focus as a heartbeat for your fast: Set yourself apart, turn from every weight, receive Christ's healing, renounce every chain, embrace your true identity, walk in Spirit-given authority, and celebrate the freedom Jesus secured for you. Let each day begin with this anchor verse—spoken out loud, prayed back to God, and woven into every choice you make that day—so that by week's end the rhythm of breakthrough is no longer an event but a lifestyle.

Guiding Points & Prayer

Note:

As you spend time in prayer, be reminded that we want God to get the glory out of our lives. As you approach the day to study, focus on these points in the text.

First Point:

Let them talk: In this season, you will have people who need a platform to expose you, demean you, or even belittle you. Do not get frustrated. The only reason they're still talking is because God is going to use them to announce your next position. Fasting teaches us to rise above the voices of doubt and accusation. Let them talk because while they speak, God is lifting your head and healing your soul.

Second Point:

That is incorrect: You do not have to receive every word they say. Far too often, people will say things to you to validate their words as weight and law in your life. You have been permitted to say that is incorrect. I serve a God that is well able and faithful to do all things. They said, there's no help for me in God—but that is incorrect. Through fasting, He's healing me, lifting my head, and proving every liar wrong with His glory. We stand on God and His Word, it is through Christ that we can, and God will.

Final Point:

You are not in this by yourself: The ploy of any enemy is to use a private situation as a public embarrassment. Anything to make you hold your head down in defeat and disgust. But there is one problem, God is with me, and he is the lifter of my head. Fasting is a reminder that even when others doubt, God surrounds me with His presence. I'm not in this alone, God is my shield, my healer, and lifter of my head. Just know that everything changes when God shows up. You must believe that God is in it with you.

Prayer:

Father, I must, I can, I will acknowledge you in all that I do. Lord, I call on your mighty name, Jehovah. To ignite in me your power and strength. Lord, as I fast, silence every voice that says there's no hope for me. Be my shield, lift my head, and heal me with the power of Your presence. Plant me in your words today, so that I might know the power of your name.

THOUGHTS:

Date : ___/___/___

_____

_____

_____

_____

_____

_____

_____

_____

_____

_____

_____

_____

_____

_____

_____

_____

_____

_____

_____

_____

_____

Fast That Breaks

Being Delivered
Through Fasting

Being Delivered Through Fasting

You know, deliverance has been shunned and downplayed for so long that we don't understand its power. Deliverance isn't just about casting something out—it's about **breaking free** from everything that's had a grip on your life. Fasting is one of the most powerful tools God gives us for breakthrough. When you fast, you're denying the flesh and putting the spirit back in charge. That shift alone begins to dismantle strongholds. Sometimes we've prayed, cried, shouted, and nothing moved. But when fasting is added, it's like spiritual dynamite—it weakens the foundation of what's been oppressing you. And know this, there are some battles that won't budge until your spirit goes deeper.

Now fasting doesn't twist God's arm; it purifies yours and brings sanctification and the ability to understand your righteousness. It's not about trying to buy your freedom; it's about *aligning with God, who is responsible to set men free*. You'd be surprised how many spiritual attacks feed off of undisciplined flesh. Lust of the flesh, fear of not being good enough, anger over what they did to you, addiction to things outside of Christ; these spirits lose access when you *crucify the flesh through fasting*. The appetite you starve stops controlling you. So, when you fast, your discernment sharpens, your spiritual strength rises, and you begin to recognize what's been hiding under emotional patterns, habits, and generational cycles. That's where real deliverance begins, when the light of God exposes what you thought was "just how you are."

Deliverance through fasting is also about regaining your authority.
You've been under too long—under pressure of life, under torment of the enemy, under the weight of things God never meant for you to carry. But when you fast, you're not just humbling yourself; you're stepping into position, a posture of authority. You begin to speak differently. You start commanding instead of begging. You declare instead of wondering. Fasting reminds the enemy and yourself, who you really are in Christ. You're not a victim. You're not stuck. You are a son of God with power, and fasting awakens that identity spiritually.

There's also something sacred about what happens during the fast. God begins to reveal the root cause and not just the fruit cause. You may have been trying to fix the behavior, but fasting will show you the wound. And that's where healing and deliverance connect. When the Holy Spirit reveals the source, whether it's rejection of people, feeling abandoned and alone, discontent and afflicted because it happened and you had no control, then the chains begin to fall off at once. And once the root is severed, the cycle breaks and can no longer be what it was. You're not just getting free for a moment, you're getting free for good, for the last time.

So, if you're feeling stuck between two seasons, bound by life and its cares, or tormented in any area, I want you to **fast with an expectation of deliverance**. Not in fear, not in weariness, but with the **full belief** that God is going to meet you at the point of your need. Your breakthrough is not far off—it's in the fast. Let every demon that's been hiding out lose its grip. Let every chain be broken in the presence of God. Because when you fast under His instruction, you won't just feel better, you'll walk out free, whole, and delivered.

Now, let's take the next 7 Days and be totally delivered through fasting.

Fasting Guide: Day Eight

Focus Scripture: Numbers 13:33

"There we saw the giants (the
descendants of Anak came from the
giants); and we were like grasshoppers in
our own sight, and so we were in their
sight."

Note:

Use this simple daily focus as a heartbeat for your fast: Set yourself apart, turn from every weight, receive Christ's healing, renounce every chain, embrace your true identity, walk in Spirit-given authority, and celebrate the freedom Jesus secured for you. Let each day begin with this anchor verse—spoken out loud, prayed back to God, and woven into every choice you make that day—so that by week's end the rhythm of breakthrough is no longer an event but a lifestyle.

Guiding Points & Prayer

Note:

As you begin your day of fasting, may toy be emptied of self, filled with power, and clothed in the fire of God's glory. As you approach the day to study, focus on these points in the text.

First Point:

See beyond it: Let's be honest, that is a tricky thing to do. Giants in your life have a way of making you look small. But do you know who you serve? You serve the God of heaven, and that is where your focus needs to be. I can do hard things with God. I can handle hard things with God. Through fasting, God often reveals internal strongholds—fear, insecurity, rejection, and unbelief. These are spiritual giants that keep us out of our promise and cause us never to see beyond it.

Second Point:

You are a tree: Did you know that small grasshoppers like to hide in large trees? So, in the midst of those giants, stand tall trees and stay rooted and connected to the vine. People's opinion of you does not even matter, so do not let what they say affect your faith. Notice how it says in the text, "We were as grasshoppers in our own sight." That's not how God saw them. Deliverance through fasting reintroduces you to who you really are. You are a child of God with dominion, authority, and power. It breaks the false image and resurrects the warrior within. We must learn to drown out the noise of others so we can see God's plan for our lives.

Final Point:

Now face your giant: Far too long, the giants won, the giants were in control. You have to let those giants rule and ruin your life far too long. But that ends now! The tides have turned. Take your authority back through Jesus Christ and win! You are the righteousness of God! Fasting confronts the giant within before it conquers the giant without. Deliverance begins when you stop running and start facing what's been keeping you bound. It does not matter that people see you as small. You are great in the sight of our heavenly Father.

Prayer:

Father God, I thank you for victory. Grant unto me the courage to take bold steps and the faith to trust in Your plan. Lord, as I fast, expose every hidden chain and break every yoke that has held me captive. Let this be the fast that brings deliverance, freedom, and divine alignment. Give me strength to know that I am a winner and with you I cannot fail.

Date : ___/___/___

_____
_____
_____
_____
_____
_____
_____
_____
_____
_____
_____
_____
_____
_____
_____
_____
_____
_____
_____
_____
_____

Fast That Breaks

Fasting Guide: Day Nine

Focus Scripture: 2 Corinthians 12:9

But he said to me, "My grace is sufficient for you, for my power is made perfect in weakness." Therefore, I will boast all the more gladly about my weaknesses so that Christ's power may rest on me.

Note:

Use this simple daily focus as a heartbeat for your fast: Set yourself apart, turn from every weight, receive Christ's healing, renounce every chain, embrace your true identity, walk in Spirit-given authority, and celebrate the freedom Jesus secured for you. Let each day begin with this anchor verse—spoken out loud, prayed back to God, and woven into every choice you make that day—so that by week's end the rhythm of breakthrough is no longer an event but a lifestyle.

Guiding Points & Prayer

Note:

As you focus on God, his favor, and blessings, be reminded that no blessing is gained without test. We all have challenges and trials to face in life. But overcoming them is what causes the blessing of God to come on us. As you approach the day to study, focus on these points in the text.

First Point:

God is more than enough: Oftentimes, the thing you need God to address or do, he does not. Paul wanted God to remove his thorn. But God's response to Paul, is the same as he responding to you, that he is more than enough. God is more than capable to handle anything that you face, anything that you go through. In fasting, you must embrace your weakness so that Christ's strength may rise within you. Through surrendering your will, deliverance flows—not by my power, but by His grace. There is nothing God cannot do.

Second Point:

God does not see what you see: We see problems, trouble, pain, storms, and sickness. God sees solutions, victory, healing, peace, and deliverance. We must change our focus to God's focus to see what he sees. God does not see you as you see yourself, he sees you through the lens of Christ. May your eyes become open during the fast, for what breaks you becomes the very place where deliverance and grace overflow.

Final Point:

Resting in Christ's power: When you know God is more than enough, and you can see what he sees, you can rest in the power Christ. Do not let these thorns carry you to weakness when you win in the end. Daily, you must lay down your strength and rest in Christ's power that delivers and sustains. His grace becomes your anchor to where your strength ends, and His victory begins.

Prayer:

God of Heaven and Earth, I pray for clarity today. Help me find contentment in the present moment and trust in Your timing. Clear my mind of confusion and grant me clarity in making Godly decisions. Father, it is in our weakness, let Your grace be our strength. Deliver us by your power that rests on us through Christ alone. Help us to stand in your will and follow your lead.

Date : ___/___/___

_____
_____
_____
_____
_____
_____
_____
_____
_____
_____
_____
_____
_____
_____
_____
_____
_____
_____
_____
_____

Fast That Breaks

Fasting Guide: Day Ten

Focus Scripture: 1 John 5:4

For everyone born of God overcomes
the world. This is the victory that has
overcome the world, even our faith.

Note:

Use this simple daily focus as a heartbeat for your fast: Set yourself apart, turn from every
weight, receive Christ's healing, renounce every chain, embrace your true identity, walk in
Spirit-given authority, and celebrate the freedom Jesus secured for you. Let each day begin
with this anchor verse—spoken out loud, prayed back to God, and woven into every choice
you make that day—so that by week's end the rhythm of breakthrough is no longer an event
but a lifestyle.

Guiding Points & Prayer

Note:
As you embrace a new day, let honor and glory be rendered to the Lord, for all that He has done. As you approach the day to study, focus on these points in the text.

First Point:

You are Christ born: You originated from God. There is no one like you. No comparison. When God sees you, he sees himself. God's intention and purpose is the reason he created you for his glory. You are God-born. And because we are born of God, this fast is not a fight for victory, but a walk in it. Deliverance is your birthright, and by faith, we overcome every chain.

Second Point:

Life is meant to be won: You have the Spirit of an overcomer in you. The problem is you do not know it. To accomplish the purpose for which God created you is to know that you win. Fasting positions, us to walk in the victory we were born to carry. Through Christ, deliverance isn't a struggle, it's the proof that I was made to win. Not sometimes, but every time.

Final Point:

Built In Faith: Understand that God requires you to know what is woven into the fabric of your life. It is your faith. Fasting activates the faith we're already built with, born of God, wired to overcome. Deliverance flows not from striving, but from the victory my faith was designed to release. It is your faith that believes in the impossible, sees the invisible, and expects the incredible.

Prayer:

Dear God, lead me to where you are. Help me to see the possibilities in every difficulty and the lessons in every trial. Thank You for the reminder that I am born of You and built to overcome. Strengthen my faith through this fast and let deliverance manifest by the victory already within me. Help me to know that with you in my life I can do all things, and nothing is impossible.

Date : ___ / ___ / ___

_____
_____
_____
_____
_____
_____
_____
_____
_____
_____
_____
_____
_____
_____
_____
_____
_____
_____
_____
_____
_____

Fast That Breaks

Fasting Guide: Day Eleven

Focus Scripture: Colossians 1:10

For everyone born of God overcomes
the world. This is the victory that has
overcome the world, even our faith.

Note:

Use this simple daily focus as a heartbeat for your fast: Set yourself apart, turn from every
weight, receive Christ's healing, renounce every chain, embrace your true identity, walk in
Spirit-given authority, and celebrate the freedom Jesus secured for you. Let each day begin
with this anchor verse—spoken out loud, prayed back to God, and woven into every choice
you make that day—so that by week's end the rhythm of breakthrough is no longer an event
but a lifestyle.

Guiding Points & Prayer

Note:
 So that you may live a life worthy of the Lord and please him in every way: bearing fruit in every good work, growing in the knowledge of God. As you approach the day to study, focus on these points in the text.

First Point:

Live Differently: The expectation of accepting Christ is to now live according to Christ. That requires us to make changes in accordance with our lifestyle. Your life must be different than when living a life of sin. Fasting sets, you apart to live a life worthy of the Lord, bearing fruit that looks like Him. Deliverance frees me to walk differently, fully pleasing God in power and purpose. Your life must be different than those around you that refuse to serve God. Your life must stand out for Christ.

Second Point:

Please Him: Our only goal is to please the Lord and the way we please him is by submitting to His authority in our lives. To many things, situations, and people come to take the place of Christ in our lives. But in pleasing Him, he reminds us of how invaluable everything else is and the value of pleasing Him. It is through fasting; we realign our lives to fully please the Lord in every good work. Deliverance clears the path so that our walk reflects His will and bears lasting fruit. Making Christ the center of your life is the key to pleasing God.

Final Point:

It is about your growth: The bottom line is that your knowledge of Christ should produce a growth in Him. You should never settle for getting enough of his word, or knowing who He is, or being in His presence. Growth takes time, patience, and the ability to deal with those areas that are unproductive. Fasting creates space for growth by cutting away what stunts our walk with God. Deliverance clears the soil so we can grow deeper in His knowledge and bear lasting fruit. As you grow in the knowledge of God, cultivation leads to the development of who Christ has called you to be.

Prayer:

Father, grant me the courage to move forward, even when the road seems tough, and challenges are hard to bare. Show me your mercy and allow me to live in your grace. Lord, as I fast, cause me to walk worthy of you and grow in every good work. Let deliverance remove all that hinders my growth, that I may fully please You. Help me to take shelter in your word.

THOUGHTS:

Date : ___/___/___

_____
_____
_____
_____
_____
_____
_____
_____
_____
_____
_____
_____
_____
_____
_____
_____
_____
_____
_____

Fast That Breaks

Fasting Guide: Day Twelve

Focus Scripture: 1 Timothy 4:12

Be thou an example of the believers, in
word, in conversation. In charity. In
spirit, in faith, in purity.

Note:

Use this simple daily focus as a heartbeat for your fast: Set yourself apart, turn from every
weight, receive Christ's healing, renounce every chain, embrace your true identity, walk in
Spirit-given authority, and celebrate the freedom Jesus secured for you. Let each day begin
with this anchor verse—spoken out loud, prayed back to God, and woven into every choice
you make that day—so that by week's end the rhythm of breakthrough is no longer an event
but a lifestyle.

Guiding Points & Prayer

Note:
As you focus on today, ask yourself the tough questions. Are you living as Christ example in the earth. As you approach the day to study, focus on these points in the text.

First Point:

Be an example: An example is not what you say, but it is according to how you live. You cannot choose when you want to be holy. Holiness is a lifestyle. That is your example. Fasting disciplines your life so you can be an example in purity, faith, and power. Deliverance frees you from what would disqualify your witness, so others see Christ in your life. Christ came that we might be imitators of him in all things.

Second Point:

You are a believer: Stand out and be different than the world. Take your instructions from God. Mirror his words, not this world. As a believer, fasting strengthens your example and deepens your level of discipline. Deliverance removes every hidden weight so that your life reflects the faith that you profess. As a believer, our job is to have an assurance that God exists, and Christ lives in us.

Final Point:

Live it: Your lifestyle is the governing factor of how you believe and what you believe. To this Point, we ought to talk differently, conduct and behave differently, how you treat others should look different, your attitude should be different, how you believe should be different, your morals are different. No one ever said that being an example is easy. Fasting helps you to crucify the flesh so you can truly live what you believe. Deliverance clears the path so that your life becomes a living example of the gospel you carry.

Prayer:

Father, grace me with strength to stand out and be who you called me to be. Fill me with the assurance that I am enough and that I can handle whatever comes my way. Father, shape me to be an example in word, conduct, and faith. Let deliverance remove every hindrance so my life testifies of Your power. I stand in your word today and I put my trust in your plan for my life.

Date : ___ / ___ / ___

_____
_____
_____
_____
_____
_____
_____
_____
_____
_____
_____
_____
_____
_____
_____
_____
_____
_____
_____
_____

Fast That Breaks

Fasting Guide: Day Thirteen

Focus Scripture: 2 Corinthians 4:17

For our light affliction, which is but for
a moment, worketh for us a far more
exceeding and eternal weight of glory.

Note:

Use this simple daily focus as a heartbeat for your fast: Set yourself apart, turn from every
weight, receive Christ's healing, renounce every chain, embrace your true identity, walk in
Spirit-given authority, and celebrate the freedom Jesus secured for you. Let each day begin
with this anchor verse—spoken out loud, prayed back to God, and woven into every choice
you make that day—so that by week's end the rhythm of breakthrough is no longer an event
but a lifestyle.

Guiding Points & Prayer

Note:
As you embrace this day of the fast, change your focus. Let us see God as the God of Promise and Provision. As you approach the day to study, focus on these points in the text.

First Point:

How heavy can it be: Heaviness is defined by how much you can carry. Christ is the one who carries the full load. We often carry the grief of it, the pain of it, the pressure of it, not realizing it is not yours to carry. Fasting helps us to endure the weight of this moment, knowing it's producing eternal glory. Deliverance reminds us that no heaviness can outweigh the power of God's hand on our lives. You have the right to be weight-less.

Second Point:

Any moment now: Do you realize how fast things can change? One answered prayer from God can turn your situation all the way around. Who says it must last this long? Get connected to the source of all things. Fasting prepares us for the glory that's about to break through—any moment now. Deliverance is near, for these light afflictions are making room for something greater. Do not just look for things to change; expect and believe things will change at any moment.

Final Point:

It's got to work: Know this, that after you have given God the burden, prayed that matter through, believed for things to change, the only thing left is for things to start working in your favor. You did not survive, only to succumb to the enemy's defeat. Fasting may feel heavy now, but it's working a far greater weight of glory. Deliverance is not a question, it's a promise in motion, and it's got to work. Your survival is proof that victory can be won. It is working for your good.

Prayer:

Father, thank you for allowing me to stand another day, walking victoriously in you. Lord, infuse me with hope and keep my heart steadfast and true. Lord, as we fast through this light aUliction, let it work in me a greater glory. Bring deliverance through what I endure and let nothing be wasted in Your process. Let Your grace be my guide, through diUiculties and remind me of Your constant presence.

Fast That Breaks

Fasting Guide: Day Fourteen

Focus Scripture: Hebrews 13:5

Keep your lives free from the love of
money and be content with what you
have, because God has said, "Never will
I leave you; never will I forsake you.

Note:

Use this simple daily focus as a heartbeat for your fast: Set yourself apart, turn from every
weight, receive Christ's healing, renounce every chain, embrace your true identity, walk in
Spirit-given authority, and celebrate the freedom Jesus secured for you. Let each day begin
with this anchor verse—spoken out loud, prayed back to God, and woven into every choice
you make that day—so that by week's end the rhythm of breakthrough is no longer an event
but a lifestyle.

Guiding Points & Prayer

Note:
As you embrace another day of the fast, let it serve as a reminder, God has not forsaken you. You are never alone. As you approach the day to study, focus on these points in the text.

First Point:

Who is your source: You cannot exist or form any tangible things and keep them without realizing where your source lies. When you make God your source, he continues to prove to us time and time again that he is faithful in all things. Fasting reminds us of that God alone is our source, not people, not possessions. Deliverance flows when I let go of what I thought I needed and trust the One who said, 'I will never leave you.'" God is not your resource; he is your source.

Second Point:

Where does your contentment lie: Fame and fortune fade, but Faith is Forever! All that you have, it came from God. All that you need, God can supply. When there is a loss of contentment, it produces feelings of dissatisfaction, bitterness, anger, frustration, and no hope. Fasting strips away false comforts to reveal where my true contentment lies, in Christ alone. Deliverance comes when I stop clinging to what I can't satisfy and rest in the One who never leaves. Whatever God provides, be content in that.

Final Point:

You are not alone in this: Dark times can bring about a feeling that you are all alone. But it is in those moments that God reveals how much he loves you. Just look around and see the faithfulness of God, the hand of God, the protection of God, the power of God. And you will be reminded that you have never been alone. Fasting may lead you into the wilderness, but never into isolation. Please know that God is with you. Deliverance is assured, because the God who promised never to leave you is fighting right beside you. So, understand that God meant this thing for the long haul. You now must commit and bring yourself to the faithfulness of a God that will always be by your side.

Prayer:

Father, give me strength to face today's challenges and courage to overcome them. Fill my heart with confidence, knowing that You believe in me. Lord, as I fast remind me that I am never alone, you are my constant help and deliverer. Let your abiding presence break every chain and anchor my soul in contentment. May Your presence lift my spirit and renew my determination.

Date : ___/___/___

_____
_____
_____
_____
_____
_____
_____
_____
_____
_____
_____
_____
_____
_____
_____
_____
_____
_____
_____
_____
_____

Fast That Breaks

Being Set Free
Through Fasting

Being Set Free Through Fasting

You know, freedom doesn't start with your circumstances, it starts within. You can be out of Egypt and still have Egypt in you. You can advise you are no longer a slave, but somehow, you still carry the ways, actions, and demeanors of being in slavery. Fasting is how God gets deep into the places we've hidden, denied, or grown numb to. This is where you invite the Spirit of God to do surgery on your soul. The cravings, the patterns, the mindsets, those things don't just break with just prayer. They have to be starved out. *Fasting weakens the flesh* so the grip of bondage can no longer hold you down another day.

You may not be struggling with visible sin, but you might still be bound by fear, insecurities, shame, rejection, or addiction. These are chains too. But here's the good news, fasting brings those things to the surface so the **Holy Ghost** can rid you of them once and for all. The devil wants you to believe that your struggle defines you. But fasting reminds your soul: That's not who I am, I'm a child of God and when your identity is restored, the enemy loses his legal access.

I get it, fasting may not feel easy, but it's *necessary* and it's *effective*. Every time you deny your flesh, you're declaring, I want to live free more than I want to feel full. You are making room for the Holy Spirit to invade your life. There are certain bondages, mental, emotional, or even spiritual that won't break until you bring your flesh under submission and partner with God on a deeper level. Fasting doesn't earn your freedom; it positions you to receive it.

Freedom is not the absence of struggle; it's the **presence of God** in the middle of it. As you fast, God begins to fill you, fill the emptiness, the trauma gaps, the soul wounds with His Word, with His truth, and with His Spirit. The more you starve the flesh, the stronger your spirit gets. And when your spirit becomes stronger than your struggle, that's when real freedom is felt and sustained.

So don't be discouraged if things surface that you didn't expect for them to. That's deliverance working and it's supposed to happen during this time. Let God finish what He started in you. Fasting isn't just a tool; it's a divine invitation to walk out of everything that's tried to own you. You are not what you've been through. You are not the addiction. You are not the cycle. You are a vessel being purified for glory. And through fasting, God is not just setting you free—He's teaching you how to stay free.

Now, let's take the next 7 Days and be totally set free through fasting.

Fasting Guide: Day Fifteen

Focus Scripture: James 1:12

Blessed is the man who remains
steadfast under trial, for when he has
stood the test he will receive the crown
of life, which God has promised to
those who love him.

Note:

Use this simple daily focus as a heartbeat for your fast: Set yourself apart, turn from every weight, receive Christ's healing, renounce every chain, embrace your true identity, walk in Spirit-given authority, and celebrate the freedom Jesus secured for you. Let each day begin with this anchor verse—spoken out loud, prayed back to God, and woven into every choice you make that day—so that by week's end the rhythm of breakthrough is no longer an event but a lifestyle.

Guiding Points & Prayer

Note:
As you embrace for another day of the fast, rest assured that God is able to keep you as promised. Rest in His grace and worry about nothing. As you approach the day to study, focus on these points in the text.

First Point:

Remain Steadfast: The identifier in this text is the fact that a trial awaits. Your position against the trial is to remain steadfast. Keep in mind that you are blessed to be able to take a stance and get battle ready, go through the trial. Fasting strengthens your endurance so you can remain steadfast under the pressure. As you hold firm, freedom is forming because the crown isn't just promised, it's being prepared. When you remain steadfast, this requires you to put your faith into action as you cling to the promises of God and his word.

Second Point:

There is a promise with your name on it: God has already predetermined certain miracles, moments in time, he has all certainties in your life mapped out. You now must remain in God's timing. That requires you to perfect your walk, build your faith, and stand on the Word of God. Fasting keeps you anchored while you endure the test, knowing freedom is in motion. There's a promise with your name on it and through steadfast faith, you will walk in it. Promises do come, but to the one that endures until the end.

Final Point:

It takes a lasting love: Do not be one that fall in and out of love with God when things do not go your way. Your love for Christ must run deep. He does not love you any less when we fail or falter. That does not change how much God loves you. Fasting draws me deeper into lasting love for the One who delivers and sustains me. True freedom is reserved for those who endure because love that lasts unlocks the crown. We must return to the sincere love of Christ, not for what he can do, but because of who He is. Christ the Lord.

Prayer:

Father, remind us of our worth and the power that we have through Your love. Thank you for the miracles, blessings, and victories we have won through you. Lord, as we fast, strengthen us to remain steadfast in love and faith. Set us free from every weight and lead us into the promises you've prepared for those who endure. Grant us the courage to move forward, even when the road seems tough. We stand today in your strength, knowing that we can and we will trust you for the rest of our lives.

_____
_____
_____
_____
_____
_____
_____
_____
_____
_____
_____
_____
_____
_____
_____
_____
_____
_____
_____
_____
_____

Fast That Breaks

Fasting Guide: Day Sixteen

Focus Scripture: John 14:9

Jesus said to him, "Have I been with
you so long, and yet you have not
known Me, Philip? He who has seen
Me has seen the Father; so how can you
say, 'Show us the Father"

Note:

Use this simple daily focus as a heartbeat for your fast: Set yourself apart, turn from every
weight, receive Christ's healing, renounce every chain, embrace your true identity, walk in
Spirit-given authority, and celebrate the freedom Jesus secured for you. Let each day begin
with this anchor verse—spoken out loud, prayed back to God, and woven into every choice
you make that day—so that by week's end the rhythm of breakthrough is no longer an event
but a lifestyle.

Guiding Points & Prayer

Note:
As you embrace this day to fast, let your heart and mind stay focus on God. Get to know God in an intimate way. As you approach the day to study, focus on these points in the text.

First Point:

His presence matters: Are you too distracted with your concerns to even notice the presence of God in your life? Too often we pray, we plead, we beg for God to take us to the next level. We never stop to enjoy the current level God has trusted us to be on. We must know that God exists in all things. Not just in tragedies, circumstances, and tough times, but he shows up in miracles, with the gift of peace, a heart of forgiveness, an example of dedication. Fasting draws us into the presence of God where true freedom is found because to see Jesus is to encounter deliverance. His presence breaks chains and transforms lives. He exists, but we must take the time to notice his existence.

Second Point:

Righting a wrong: You will notice in the text that Jesus is speaking specifically to Phillip. Having Jesus speak is good but having him speak directly to you makes it personal. It's our wrongs what needs corrected. Lord, show us where we've made mistakes, tell us what we need to change, show us the things we need to let go of, teach us how to forgive, show us where our shortcomings are. Fasting brings us face to face with Jesus. In His presence, lies are broken, truth is revealed, and freedom begins to flow. No more arbitrary words, I want to live my life and hear from my father.

Final Point:

A Visible Father: Since when does the father hide himself? He cannot, the only way to see him is to seek him with your whole heart. In order to seek God with your whole heart, we must open our hearts and allow God to see what's in it. See my brokenness, see my doubts, see my pain, see my hurt, see my hidden sins, see my false truths, see my fears. Fasting opens our eyes to see the Father revealed in Christ, the One who never hides in our struggle. In His visible presence, I'm not only seen, but I am set free. There is nothing wrong with exposing your heart to God. After the exposure comes the visibility of God, to see what He sees.

Prayer:

Lord God, I am honored to call you Father. Thank you for the continued love and grace you give me each day. Bless this new day and the opportunities it holds. Lord, as I fast, reveal the Father to my heart through the face of Jesus. Let Your presence break every chain and set me free by the power of who You are. May my life be filled with Your guidance and grace. Teach me to be humble and to recognize that all good things come from You.

Date : ___ / ___ / ___

_____
_____
_____
_____
_____
_____
_____
_____
_____
_____
_____
_____
_____
_____
_____
_____
_____
_____
_____

Fast That Breaks

Fasting Guide: Day Seventeen

Focus Scripture: Ecclesiastes 11:5

As you do not know the way the spirit
comes to the bones in the womb of a
woman with child, so you do not know
the work of God who makes
everything."

Note:

Use this simple daily focus as a heartbeat for your fast: Set yourself apart, turn from every weight, receive Christ's healing, renounce every chain, embrace your true identity, walk in Spirit-given authority, and celebrate the freedom Jesus secured for you. Let each day begin with this anchor verse—spoken out loud, prayed back to God, and woven into every choice you make that day—so that by week's end the rhythm of breakthrough is no longer an event but a lifestyle.

Guiding Points & Prayer

Note:

As you embrace another day to fast, shift your mind to know that everything comes from the Lord, it is He who has made heaven and earth. As you approach the day to study, focus on these points in the text.

First Point:

When it is, we just don't know: Have you ever not known the direction God was taking you or the plan that was for your life? How long will the pain, struggle, storm, hurt, difficulty, or even the sorrow last? How long will it last until you come out to the place of promise? You may never understand the full details of God's intimate plans. Fasting teaches us how to trust what we cannot trace, knowing God is working in mystery. Even when we don't know when, we know freedom is forming in the unseen. Just like no one can fathom how God takes a seed and forms a being, he is also the God who takes your faith and delivers on his promise.

Second Point:

He is working it out: It is what you cannot see that is working for what you will see. Having faith in dark times of uncertainty can be a challenge, but it is a requirement to please God. To understand it is working, you must believe it works. Fasting reminds us that even in silence, God is still at work behind the veil. Though we can't see how, he is working out our freedom with divine precision. This is not the time to lose faith in God over what you cannot see. But have hope in God according to what you will see.

Final Point:

God, our maker: God made all things for his purpose, his timing, in his glory. It is not up to you or me to figure God out; it is up to us to follow him. When we stop trying to figure things out, you will realize that things have already been worked out by God, our maker. Position yourself to follow his word, be led by his spirit, and we will end up in the place that has already been promised. Fasting returns us to the hands of our Maker, who shapes freedom in ways we can't explain. He formed us in mystery, and in that same mystery, he sets us free. Do not get this far and forget that God, our maker, can still do all things promised.

Prayer:

Father, we are so grateful for your undivided love for us. Infuse our day with joy and remind us to find happiness in the little things. Guide our thoughts and actions so we may face challenges with grace and confidence. Father, as we fast, we trust you as my Maker working in ways we cannot see. Set us free according to Your wisdom, not our own understanding. Lord, may we forever trust your will and look forward to the promises of your word.

_____

_____

_____

_____

_____

_____

_____

_____

_____

_____

_____

_____

_____

_____

_____

_____

_____

_____

_____

Fasting Guide: Day Eighteen

Focus Scripture: Psalms 27:4

One thing I have desired of the Lord,
that will I seek after; that I may dwell in
the house of the Lord all the days of my
life, to behold the beauty of the Lord,
and to enquire in his temple.

Note:

Use this simple daily focus as a heartbeat for your fast: Set yourself apart, turn from every weight, receive Christ's healing, renounce every chain, embrace your true identity, walk in Spirit-given authority, and celebrate the freedom Jesus secured for you. Let each day begin with this anchor verse—spoken out loud, prayed back to God, and woven into every choice you make that day—so that by week's end the rhythm of breakthrough is no longer an event but a lifestyle.

Guiding Points & Prayer

Note:
As you embrace another day of the fast, let your heart and mind stay committed to the things of God. As you approach the day to study, focus on these points in the text.

First Point:

The one thing: According to the text, David's top priority in life was his relationship with the Lord. That one thing became the most important thing. What is most important to you? Having the finer things of life, making It to the top of success, what happens when those things never fulfill the desire anymore? Fasting brings our heart back to the one thing that matters and that is dwelling in His presence. In that place, every chain breaks and true freedom begins to rise. In you, God has placed a desire for himself. It is up to us to make his desire become our desire. It is that one thing.

Second Point:

What do you really want? Anything you want, you go after. David said the thing I want; I am not going to stop till I get it. That is called passion, which is called hunger, which is called delight. What do you really want? Do you want his hand, or do you want him, do you want what He can do for you, or do you want him, do you want what he has to offer you, or do you want him? Fasting reveals the true desires of our heart and realigns us with what matters most and that is his presence. When you want Him more than freedom itself, that's when freedom finds you. Cause wanting him is a desire for him that you never stop going after.

Final Point:

The Destination: David said I want to dwell in the presence of the Lord. Now, we have been in the presence of people, and nothing has changed, we have even been in the presence of things, and they have done nothing for us. But in the presence of God, there is a fullness of joy, a peace that only he can give, a satisfaction that completes our waning soul. It is the destination I am after because once I get there, I never have to leave, I never have to worry, I am never left to be alone. Fasting reminds us that His presence is not just the journey, it's the destination. True freedom is found not in what I leave behind, but in where I choose to dwell. It is the destination of his presence that I am after to abide with him forever.

Prayer:

Father, in you I put my trust, let not my heart faint, but let me be steadfast in your love and guidance. May Your support be my anchor and Your love be my motivation to remain in your will. Lord, as we fast, let my one desire be to dwell in Your presence. Set us free in the place where we behold Your beauty and find our true home. We love dwelling in your presence, may we forever find strength, grace, peace, and the willingness to trust you forever.

Fast That Breaks

Fasting Guide: Day Nineteen

Focus Scripture: 1 Timothy 6:12

Fight the good fight of faith. Take hold
of the eternal life to which you were
called when you made your good
confession in the presence of many
witnesses.

Note:

Use this simple daily focus as a heartbeat for your fast: Set yourself apart, turn from every
weight, receive Christ's healing, renounce every chain, embrace your true identity, walk in
Spirit-given authority, and celebrate the freedom Jesus secured for you. Let each day begin
with this anchor verse—spoken out loud, prayed back to God, and woven into every choice
you make that day—so that by week's end the rhythm of breakthrough is no longer an event
but a lifestyle.

Guiding Points & Prayer

Note:
As you embrace this day of the fast, remember you do not have to be the fastest, just finish the race. As you approach the day to study, focus on these points in the text.

First Point:

Fight for what you believe: In Paul talking to Timothy in the text, he was encouraging him to be on guard against the varied doctrines, teachings, beliefs, and false knowledge that comes against the Word of God and your faith in God. But us that are in Christ Jesus, we know the truth, so we are responsible to guard, to protect, and to adhere to the standards of God's word. Fasting strengthens your spirit to fight the good fight of faith with focus and fire. Freedom doesn't come by feeling, it comes by contending for what we believe. This will result in you taking a defensive stance in what you believe. God does not need protection, but he needs us to guard his word so we can keep it until the end.

Second Point:

The fight is for eternal: When we guard our life and take charge of God's word, we do this in order to receive eternal life. What is prohibiting you from fighting to the eternal? Spiritually, we have let our guard down. Society has taken the voice of God and given you their thoughts, their opinions, their views on your spiritual life. Fasting reminds us that this fight is not for comfort, but for the eternal call on our lives. Being set free is not just about now, it's about finishing in victory where it counts forever. What they say comes with no fight and does not lead to eternal. It is time to contend for the faith.

Final Point:

Make your confession last: It is one thing to make your confession to God, but it is another to make your confession to many witnesses. Your reward is not based on how many witnesses see you, but how many can you win to Christ. You must keep fighting so that Christ may be seen and visible in the earth. This is where perseverance comes in. To last is to finish. Fasting strengthens the faith behind your confession, so it doesn't fade in the fight. Deliverance empowers us to live what we've declared until the end. This is not the time to give up, you must endure until the end.

Prayer:

Father, you are my strong tower, you made me become righteous. When I am weak, you remain strong. When life is hard, you face it with me. Lord, as I fast, strengthen me to fight the good fight of faith with endurance and truth. Set me free from every hindrance so my confession remains strong until the end. When nights are long and days are weary, you provide shelter in your arms. Let me rest in your guidance and contend for the faith.

_____
_____
_____
_____
_____
_____
_____
_____
_____
_____
_____
_____
_____
_____
_____
_____
_____
_____
_____
_____

Fasting Guide: Day Twenty

Focus Scripture: Matthew 12:29

Or how can one enter a strong man's house and plunder his goods, unless he first binds the strong man? And then he will plunder his house.

Note:

Use this simple daily focus as a heartbeat for your fast: Set yourself apart, turn from every weight, receive Christ's healing, renounce every chain, embrace your true identity, walk in Spirit-given authority, and celebrate the freedom Jesus secured for you. Let each day begin with this anchor verse—spoken out loud, prayed back to God, and woven into every choice you make that day—so that by week's end the rhythm of breakthrough is no longer an event but a lifestyle.

Guiding Points & Prayer

Note:
As you embrace this day to fast, you must know that God's has given us authority and activation. As you approach the day to study, focus on these points in the text.

First Point:

Take back your house: Too many of us as believers have taken on the Spirit of fear and have let the enemy come in and not just take the house but keep the house. And it is evident because fear comes with no strength, no resilience, no hope, what is the use because nothing is ever going to change. But the Bible declares just the opposite, that God did not you a spirit of fear, but that of power, love, and a sound mind. Notice what God gave you, Power! Fasting is how we bind the strong man and take back the house the enemy tried to occupy. Deliverance restores what was stolen because this house belongs to God. What God gives you will always defeat the enemy. You have been given authority by God, so take back the house.

Second Point:

It does not belong to the strongman: Most of what the enemy does and takes from us; he does so in our ignorance and our lack of knowing who God is. So many things of ours are in the enemy's possession. The problem is, it does not belong to him, it belongs to you, the righteous. Fasting declares that my life, my mind, and my house do not belong to the strongman. Through deliverance, I reclaim what the enemy tried to possess because it's God's territory. It is time to take back your peace, take back your joy, take back your authority, take back your passion, take back your life in God. It does not belong to the strongman.

Guiding Points & Prayer

Continued

Note:

As you embrace this day to fast, you must know that God's has given us authority and activation. As you approach the day to study, focus on these points in the text.

Final Point:

The Correct Owner: In looking at this text, Jesus was not just teaching authority, but he was also teaching ownership. This is your house, not that it was, **but it is** your house. Just because a strongman has taken over your house does not mean it changes who the correct owner Is. The house is still deeded and titled to you. That gives you all rights, access, and privileges to that house. You are the owner. Fasting breaks the false claim of the strongman and restores authority to the rightful owner. Deliverance confirms that this house belongs to Christ, not the enemy.

It is not time to sell, it is time to evict every spirit, every enemy, every principality out of the house. The righteous are in authority and the people shall rejoice.

Prayer:

Father, it is in you we put our faith. Let Your grace guide us through difficulties and remind us of Your constant presence. Watch over us and our loved ones, keeping us safe and secure. Lord, as we fast, bind every strongman that has occupied what belongs to us. Set us free and reestablish Your rightful ownership over every part of our lives. May you forever be Lord of our lives. We stand in your righteous authority, to know that we are victorious, you made us win.

Date : ___/___/___

_____
_____
_____
_____
_____
_____
_____
_____
_____
_____
_____
_____
_____
_____
_____
_____
_____
_____
_____
_____
_____

Fasting Guide: Day Twenty One

Focus Scripture: John 15:7

If you abide in me, and my words abide
in you, ask whatever you wish, and it
will be done
for you.

Note:

Use this simple daily focus as a heartbeat for your fast: Set yourself apart, turn from every weight, receive Christ's healing, renounce every chain, embrace your true identity, walk in Spirit-given authority, and celebrate the freedom Jesus secured for you. Let each day begin with this anchor verse—spoken out loud, prayed back to God, and woven into every choice you make that day—so that by week's end the rhythm of breakthrough is no longer an event but a lifestyle.

Guiding Points & Prayer

Note:
As you embrace this last day of the fast, I pray that you feel encouraged that God has given us Authority and Activation to win every battle. We stand complete in Christ Jesus. As you approach the day to study, focus on these points in the text.

First Point:

It's Conditional: This is an inventory text. Have you checked to see what is abiding in you? The word abide means to live, to dwell, to hide, to remain. So, are you abiding in Christ? What's your position in Christ? Do you stand in the seat of faith? Are you resting in his grace? Is Christ your hope? Does the love of God dwell in you? Fasting positions, us to abide deeply, because freedom flows where His Word lives in us. Deliverance is not automatic; it's released when we meet the condition of abiding. If you answer no to these questions, you won't meet the conditions. God is not a conditional God; he is a continual God. So, you must continually abide in him to meet the conditions.

Second Point:

Word in, Word out: This is where training comes in. We must eat the word, get full on it, digest it, and eat it again. Have you eaten the word or have you just tasted the word? The more Word you consume, you have no choice but to abide. The world says consuming too much of something is not good for you. On the other hand, a large consumption of the word produces fruit that will remain. Fasting clears the noise so the Word can dwell richly within, word in, freedom out. Deliverance comes when His Word becomes our weapon and our way. Fruits of joy, peace, happiness, hope, and sanctification. Consume less of the world and more of the word of God.

Guiding Points & Prayer

Continued

Note:

As you embrace this last day of the fast, I pray that you feel encouraged that God has given us Authority and Activation to win every battle. We stand complete in Christ Jesus. As you approach the day to study, focus on these points in the text.

Final Point:

What are you about to receive: Everything in Christ is already complete, its already done, it cannot be changed. So, from the moment the consumption of God's word is made in you, you are immediately brought into a place of completion. So, to ask God anything is knowing that what I am asking is already done, I am now able to receive. Fasting prepares the soil of my soul to receive what abiding has positioned me for. When His Word lives in us, deliverance is not just possible, it's inevitable. We often ask from a place of need verses a place of Christ has already done it. You and I have been positioned to receive everything in Christ. Our healing, our deliverance, our door, our provision, our future. It's done and that's worthy of praise.

Prayer:

My Lord and God. Strengthen my faith in Your plan and help me to trust in Your wisdom and timing. Lord, guide my steps today and illuminate the path I should follow. Help me to cultivate patience and understanding, both with others and with myself. Lord, as I fast and abide in You, let Your Word abide richly in me. Release deliverance as I align my desires with Your will and walk in Your truth. Grant me the courage to take bold steps and the faith to trust in Your plan.

Date : ___/___/___

_____

_____

_____

_____

_____

_____

_____

_____

_____

_____

_____

_____

_____

_____

_____

_____

_____

_____

_____

_____

_____

Fast That Breaks

Being Healed, Being Delivered, Being Set Free

Fasting is where you stop running and let God deal with the places in you that no one sees. It's not about impressing God with sacrifice; it's about inviting Him into the war happening beneath the surface. You may not know how to fix it, but He does. When you fast, you're not just pushing away food, you're pulling heaven closer to you. Fasting is where the Spirit begins to whisper truth into the lies you've believed, and suddenly, things that use to control you begin to lose their power and ability to control your life.

Fasting is sacred because it slows you down long enough for God to speak. Many people are carrying silent injuries, internal fractures masked by smiles and busy schedules. But when you fast, the Holy Spirit walks you back to the place of the wound, not to relive it, but to restore what was broken. He'll touch the trauma, the abuse, the secret to much to discuss, and He won't leave you there to figure it out. Healing through fasting is deep and layered. It's the kind of restoration that makes you whole and complete in Christ.

It's not always about loud moments or dramatic manifestations. Sometimes, deliverance looks like peace where there used to be torment. Through fasting, you are no longer feeding what once fed on you. Spirits of fear, lust, anxiety, rejection, they start losing access because fasting shuts the door of agreement. When you starve the flesh, the strongholds begin to crumble. What had permission in your weakness now faces eviction by your obedience. This is how bondages are broken without you having to break down.

Being set free through fasting means God rewrites how you walk, how you think, and how you choose. You come out of the fast not just lighter in your body, but heavier in the Spirit. The residue of your past loses its voice. You begin to walk with the clarity and conviction of someone who knows they're no longer bound. The chains didn't just break—they lost their value and their ability to hold you another day. Fasting helps you divorce what was familiar but equip you to walk in a new rhythm of grace and spiritual authority.

This is your moment to confront what has followed you for too long. This is where God doesn't just pull you out, He establishes you. There's healing for the ache ,deliverance for the war, and freedom that's not momentary, but maintained. When you fast like this, you won't come out the same. Your language will shift. Your appetite will change. And what used to own you will no longer recognize you because you've been marked by the presence of a God who heals, delivers, and makes all things new.

CLOSING

FROM THE DESK OF BISHOP CALVIN M. BLAKE II:

There comes a moment in every believer's life when something within cries out for more—more clarity, more power, more of God's presence. That's when we're invited into the sacred rhythm of fasting and praying. It's not just a discipline—it's an art form. The art of fasting and praying is about leaning into divine stillness, where God becomes louder than every distraction, appetite, or war in your soul. It's where your spirit begins to breathe again, where your heart softens, and where heaven starts to invade the hidden rooms of your life. I didn't learn this overnight. I learned it in the trenches—on my knees, when I was desperate enough to say, "Lord, I don't just want a breakthrough —I need to become someone new."

Fasting and praying will change your entire life—if you let it. It's not a diet, and it's not a performance. It's an invitation to transformation. When you fast, you confront your flesh; when you pray, you connect with God. Together, they become a supernatural engine that purifies the soul, sharpens your vision, and breaks the back of cycles that have held you hostage. The internal tug-of-war begins to quiet. Bitterness lifts. Shame loses its grip. And in the place of struggle, peace shows up. When you fast and pray, you are no longer a reactor to life's pressures—you become a responder to the Spirit's whisper. I've watched God heal hearts, restore families, and open impossible doors— because someone dared to consecrate these days as holy.

So, if you're stepping into these 21 days, let them be more than a challenge, let them be your catalyst for change. Don't fast out of obligation fast with expectation. Pray like you know God is about to rearrange the very framework of your future. This is a divine setup for your deliverance, your healing, and your alignment with purpose. What if everything you've been waiting for is already in motion, and these 21 days are the bridge between where you've been and where you're finally called to walk? Don't treat these days casually—treat them prophetically. Because what starts as a private sacrifice will end with a public shift.

Date : ___/___/___

_____
_____
_____
_____
_____
_____
_____
_____
_____
_____
_____
_____
_____
_____
_____
_____
_____
_____
_____
_____
_____
_____

Fast That Breaks

Fast That Breaks

Date : ___ / ___ / ___

_____
_____
_____
_____
_____
_____
_____
_____
_____
_____
_____
_____
_____
_____
_____
_____
_____
_____
_____
_____
_____

Fast That Breaks

Date : ___/___/___

_____

_____

_____

_____

_____

_____

_____

_____

_____

_____

_____

_____

_____

_____

_____

_____

_____

_____

_____

_____

Fast That Breaks

Date : ___ / ___ / ___

_____
_____
_____
_____
_____
_____
_____
_____
_____
_____
_____
_____
_____
_____
_____
_____
_____
_____
_____
_____
_____

Fast That Breaks

ABOUT THE AUTHOR

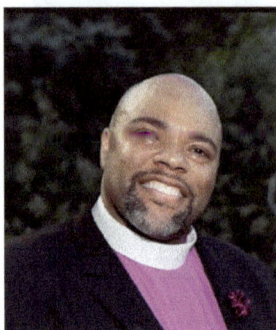

Calvin M. Blake II has faithfully served in ministry for over 23 years. He is Bishop & Founder of The Worship Center, Inc., a Christ-centered ministry in Marietta, GA. A local church dedicated to transforming lives through the Word of God, strengthening families, and impacting the community for the Kingdom of God.

Carrying forward the legacy of his late father, Calvin M. Blake Sr., Calvin is passionate about raising up disciples who make a difference in their families, communities, and beyond. Known for his dynamic preaching and engaging illustrated sermons, Calvin combines humor, depth, and practical wisdom to reach hearts across all walks of life. He has formal education in Pastoral and Biblical studies and built a successful 20+ year career in the electric industry centered around customer engagement before transitioning into healthcare management and access. His leadership blends professional excellence with a deep commitment to spiritual growth and outreach.

Outside the pulpit, he treasures time with his wife. Calvin has been married to his beloved wife, Mary, for nearly 25 years, and together they will celebrate their silver anniversary next year. Their marriage is a living testimony of love, partnership, and faith in God's design for family. A devoted father to their daughter, Krystal, and son, Isaiah, and a proud grandfather to their grandson, Jayce. Calvin's life reflects his passion for serving others and equipping believers to walk in faith, purpose, and power.